The Love of
RUGBY

Edited by   PETER WALKER

Foreword by   BILL McLAREN

CONTENTS

Half title: A game's destiny hangs in the balance. Bevan Wilson the All Black full back kicking the first of his two penalty goals in the 4th Test match, New Zealand v British Lions, Eden Park, Auckland 1977.

Endpapers: 'Wear your colours proud'. French supporters at Twickenham 1975 when their team won a high scoring game 27-20.

Title: The web-footed Sid Going (9) in his element after a cloudburst had turned Eden Park into a lake, New Zealand v Scotland, Auckland 1975.

Contents: The amazing Gareth Edwards—not in his usual red shirt of Wales or the British Lions but early in his international career, playing for a combined England and Wales team against Ireland and Scotland, October 1970.

First published 1980 by
Octopus Books Limited
59 Grosvenor Street
London W1

©1980 Octopus Books Limited
ISBN 0 7064 1229 X

Produced by Mandarin Publishers Limited
22a Westlands Road
Quarry Bay, Hong Kong
Printed in Hong Kong

Ireland's Mike Gibson

FOREWORD

That great Border and Scottish forward stalwart of the thirties, Jack Waters of Selkirk, was telling me not so long ago about the British Lions tour of South Africa in 1938 in which he played in the final test match which (to the surprise of all) the Lions won by 21-16. Jack recalled that when Charles Grieve dropped the goal that gave the Lions a timely 18-16 lead, the referee was unsure of whether the ball had cleared the bar but South African players nearer the posts unhesitatingly held their arms aloft to signify the goal.

Cynics will tell you that such sporting goodwill is a thing of the past. Yet in 1973 much the same thing happened when Scotland played Ireland at Murrayfield. The match was delicately poised at 16-14 to Scotland with time fading when Douglas Morgan dropped for goal from a lineout. No one was sure whether the decisive kick dropped over or under the bar except that favourite son of Cork, Tom Kiernan, the Irish captain. He was in no doubt and up went his left arm to signal that the kick was good.

No one would deny that certain changes have taken place in the Rugby Union game to cause concern about its future—changes in attitudes, field discipline, terracing behaviour, professionalism and in the demands made on the leisure time of players and especially those with a particular talent that sets them apart. There can be no doubt that the Rugby Union game is entering an age of challenge to its traditions and structure and that its chief administrators will have to be brave, honest and faithful in holding fast to the best of the past whilst proving far-seeing enough to embrace all that is beneficial from the present and future. The game deserves first-class management as it provides a place for all, whether large or small, short or tall, quick or slow, offering a unique camaraderie through happy socialising as well as continuing to hold out a shining example in these days of over-paid, moaning super-stars, and, of its continuing requirement for participants to accept the rough with the smooth.

I may be biased, and some might claim, blinkered, but I believe that despite modern pressures exerted by, not least, nationalistic feelings and a much wider range of competition at all levels that makes winning, to some, almost all that matters, Rugby Union men still emerge as unique sportsmen with a firm grasp still on the true sporting spirit of a tough, physical contact game.

That aspect makes me intensely proud of the game and is one which I have always been able to hold out truthfully to the young schoolboys I coach. It is a pride that was nurtured on a diet of rugged Scottish Border forward play for as a boy of eight, nine and ten years of age, I idolised such all-time, raw-boned Scottish greats as Jock Beattie (Hawick), Jock Allan (Melrose), Jimmy Graham (Kelso), Jack Waters and Willie Welsh (Hawick). As a goggle-eyed 14-year-old,

I saw Scotland win their Triple Crown and Champion-ship in a scintillating 21-16 win over England one sun-drenched March afternoon at Twickenham in 1938. As they haven't enjoyed such success since, perhaps I might be forgiven after a quarter of a century of BBC commentary work in which I have covered some 160 internationals, for having as my one remaining ambition a desire to be 'on the air' when Scotland next win the Triple Crown. They'll have to get a move on!

Rugby Union internationals provide very distinctive spectacles and some stay vivid in the memory. Curiously, one that seems etched in my mind forever was the 1963 Scotland v Wales match at Murrayfield—and it was the worst match I have ever covered because it had 111 lineouts. It's true—111. It just was a war of attrition up and down the touchlines and I remember thinking then that the game, as a spectacle, was dying. Yet what a testimony to Rugby Union's power of survival that soon it was transformed through law changes and coaching into once again, a spectator, as well as a player, sport. Thus the 1971 International Championship series was quite enthralling throughout in the tension it generated and the brilliant quality of play. I rate the Scotland v Wales match at Murrayfield that year as the finest I have ever seen even allowing for John Taylor's winning touchline conversion in a fantastic Welsh closing rally! That 1971 Welsh team rates alongside the 1951-52 Springboks and the 1967 All-Blacks as the best I have ever seen.

Yet the internationals are only the icing on the cake. The game brings such a wealth of incentive and pleasure to so many thousands and, not least, to those youngsters just stepping over the threshold of Rugby experience. Perhaps my highest satisfaction in the game derives from my donning the mantle of teacher of physical education as organiser of four primary schools matches, one of which I referee, in our local public park in Hawick on most Saturday mornings. The range of Rugby Union's attraction also was underlined on one occasion when, by sheer chance on my way to an important club game, I came across a match played by a number of overweight and over-age contestants. It was like watching a dream sequence in the pace of play and there was a tendency to boot the ball deliber-ately over the wall in order to engineer a rest period. But those lads were supremely contented to be enjoying what was, for them, a game. All of which surely shows that it is, indeed, a super game, as truely reflected in this marvellous book.

Bill McLaren 1980

ENGLAND
A half back wilderness

The very name of the game is Rugby football, because it took that name from the code of football played at Rugby School in Warwickshire in the early part of the 19th century. Part of the legend of the game has it that a boy called William Webb Ellis, who later became a parson, first took a football in his arms and ran with it, in the year 1823, 'thus originating the distinctive feature of the Rugby game'. Those words are engraved on a stone tablet built into the wall between Rugby School and the field known as Big Side, where the boys played football, and if you accept them at their face value, they tell not only the story of the origin of Rugby football in England, but also throughout the world itself.

History, however, is rarely as tidy as that, and it is not so in this case. The playing of football goes back

Below: A portrait of William Webb Ellis who, as a schoolboy, was instrumental in the development of Rugby football. Ironically, after starting the game in England he now lies buried in the South of France. Even he could not have imagined Rugby's growth throughout the world.

Right: The determination of Andy Ripley; France v England Paris 1974, a game which ended in a 12-12 draw. The 6' 5" back row forward was a terrifying sight to any would be defender. At his best when going forward, but during his peak England were invariably on the retreat.

to the annual national coaching course, he has among his priorities the fostering of mini-rugby in the eight to 12 age group, midi-rugby for those between 12 and 16 and youth rugby at under 18 and under 21 level. I would be prepared to wager that he will soon have an assistant for there is much to be done at the older levels to complement the encouraging growth of mini-rugby.

The SRU attitude to the Fourth Estate was embodied for many in the location of the press box at Murrayfield which, it was once bitterly remarked, could hardly have been farther from the pitch and still be included in the solar system. Moreover, when they at last decided that they would have to appoint a Public Relations Officer they kept that particular news item strictly to themselves. More recently, however, they have made a much greater effort to live with the media to the mutual benefit of both, although they are still not too hot on medical bulletins. The supposition is still that even if a player in the Scotland XV had a leg amputated on the Thursday, he would be classified only as slightly doubtful for the Saturday. So popular has the game become that Internationals at Murrayfield are now almost entirely all-ticket, an alteration in policy having been made after 104,000 paid for admission in the Welsh match of 1976 with thousands more being turned away or giving up all hope of gaining entry after seeing, either live or on television, the scenes inside and outside the ground. Mark you, even as long ago as that memorable Welsh match of 1951, there were tales of gates being torn down and thousands had to be seated on the grass around the pitch. It was also rumoured that many Welshmen, having been in Edinburgh all week and perhaps no longer quite at their best, had dutifully followed the crowd wending its way out to the match, only to find themselves, to their considerable surprise, at Tynecastle with the Hearts, not Wales, on the field!

There have always been names in Scottish rugby which caught the imagination of the public. The late Wilson Shaw is an obvious example. Even so, the season after his *tour de force* at Twickenham and Scotland's Triple Crown triumph of 1938, the little fly half with the blistering acceleration found himself shunted into his country's threequarter line as Scotland went from winning all three to losing all three. This move reflected the kind of maddening selectorial zig-zag which has so often ravaged Scotland's frequently limited resources.

Yet never have rugby players been such household names as Ian McLauchlan and Andy Irvine in this television era: not even in the Grand Slam days of the 'Oxford three-quarter line' among them Ian Smith, the

the confines of the International Championship, into a perenially all-conquering nation. England will still enjoy a huge numerical advantage, Wales already has a wonderful club structure with a small nucleus of clubs enviably close geographically and Ireland have long had an abundance of competitive club rugby of their own, if not on a national basis. If the Leagues stop Scotland falling further behind and then allow them to hold their own, they will assuredly have justified the more rational expectations.

In the Borders, rugby was always a classless game of the people; but in Scotland as a whole those who did not advance the claims of Association Football as the national game would have plumped for golf. Now rugby has been democratized and no-one can now assert that North of the Border it is the sport of any one class or, as used to be alleged, of the Old School tie. In Scotland, as in other countries, the powers-that-be have come to see that the changes in the educational world mean that they can no longer leave it to the schoolmasters to keep up the supply of players. In the context of club rugby, the very word 'coach' used to be regarded by many as about the nastiest five-letter word in the language; even when Scotland appointed Bill Dickinson as coach they called him 'Adviser to the 1971 captain'.

Yet, as was to happen in the case of the Leagues, once they had accepted the need to introduce some kind of coaching network at senior level, the SRU did their best to make it a success. John Roxburgh, as the SRU's Technical Administrator and therefore the approximate counterpart of Don Rutherford in England and John Dawes in Wales, has been in office five years. In addition

Flying Scot, remains International rugby's record try-scorer with 23.

Standing only five foot nine inches 'on the kerb in his studs', the squat, four-square Ian McLaughlan was rightly and admiringly described by Dr Danie Craven as 'a rugby freak'. Endowed with an almost subterranean centre of gravity, 'Mighty Mouse' first made his name when, by sheer technique, he propelled more than one mountainous enemy prop through the roof of a scrum on the 1971 Lions New Zealand tour.

He has always seen the set pieces of scrum and lineout, propping and blocking as his speciality, but has otherwise often been unconventional in his interpretation of the tight head prop's role. Yet he has laid many a winning ruck on the peel or otherwise, typically slipping the ball back between his legs to provide the possession for the winning score as when Scotland won at Twickenham in 1971 for the first time in 33 years.

A soccer player until almost into his teens and a threequarter in his years at school, Andy Irvine was but sketchily schooled in the basics of full back play when he first burst upon senior rugby in Scotland as a player of electrifying verve and swerve. A lengthy goal-kicker, destined to bag his share of records at a time in the game when the proliferation of penalty kicks admittedly undermines the validity of such scoring feats, Irvine set a new world record for a full back in International rugby when he scored his seventh try from that berth in the match against France in the spring of 1978. This milestone came in the same year as he led his club to the Scottish championship. He has twice figured on the wing in a Test match for the 1974 Lions in South Africa and there

have always been those who contended that Scotland would be better fielding him in the threequarter line with a more traditional full back in the No. 15 jersey. But the essence of the counter-argument has always been that it is agonizingly difficult for the defence to 'pick him up' when he erupts from full back at a time and place of his own choosing. Astonishingly, he is the eighth full back to be capped from his school. The extraordinary procession of these FP Internationals prompted one of my favourite post-prandial remarks—to wit, when Arthur Stepney rose to his feet and introduced himself as one of that 'fast-diminishing band of Herioters' who have not played full back for their country.

In 1972 and 1973 the SRU celebrated their centenary and enterprisingly marked it with a magnificent spectacle in the form of an International sevens tournament at Murrayfield. England won. The staging of such an event was a nice touch since seven-a-side rugby was one version of the game which Scotland indisputably gave to the world.

The Melrose tournament has always retained a place all its own in the abbreviated game and one of my own fondest memories of that centenary year remains the reception given for the rugby men by the military in Edinburgh Castle. Alex Brown, once a gifted, ball-playing fly half, with Heriot's FP and Scotland but by then an SRU dignitary, hove to opposite a splendid uniformed, figure, glittering with an array of medals almost worthy of General Amin. 'I see,' said Alex Brown, sympathetically, 'you don't have a Melrose one . . .'. Despite its recent lack of success on the International field, Scottish rugby has not lost its sense of humour!

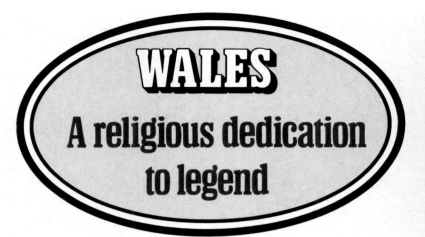

WALES
A religious dedication to legend

The sporting Welsh are a schizophrenic nation: outwardly jolly, singing extroverts with the mischievous eye and ready quip; but behind the laughter, mistrusting introverted zealots who glory in martyrdom. Paradoxically this very mixture gives a clue to why, particularly in the last decade Wales have been the dominant force in British rugby. The quicksilver mind and feet of Gerald Davies, J. J. Williams, Gareth Edwards, Barry John and Phil Bennett come from the more effervescent side of the national personality. What translates this inner ability into rugby genius is the desire of the little man, the outsider if you like, to prove himself the equal of anyone across the borders of Offa's Dyke and beyond across the seas. The Irish forwards may be demonic, the South African and New Zealand packs massive, but no other XV in the world plays with quite the same intensity of national feeling each time it takes the field as do the Welsh. With a nation's happiness and well-being resting on the shoulders of those 15 men of Wales, is it surprising that each and every one of the team is prepared to immolate himself when the whistle blows?

Wales is a vast country, not geographically of course, but in terms of the ideals and aspirations of the three million people scattered across its hills and valleys. To all intents and purposes, Wales as a rugby nation exists in the Southern coastline strip which stretches 70 miles between Newport in the east and Llanelli in the west. The catchment area extends inland some 20 miles to the heads of the valleys where the steel towns of Ebbw Vale and Tredegar provide a natural barrier to the many and varied valleys which run down to the sea in the Bristol channel. The overwhelming demands on manpower made by the coal and iron industries in the latter part of the 18th and 19th centuries has left today's South Welsh population of nearly two million a legacy of sweated labour, a strong feeling of interdependence and a close-knit resolution in facing the most appalling social deprivation: all factors which have materially influenced the Welsh philosophy on and

Right: A typical bullocking charge by Derek Quinnell, the Llanelli, Wales and British Lion all-purpose forward. Quinnell made his mark on the 1971 Lions tour and helped the Lions to become the first British side to win a series there. Somewhat injury prone, a natural by product of his whole hearted approach, Quinnell is a fine motivator in any side.

off the rugby field. It is hardly surprising, with so many Williams, Jones, Evans, Edwards and Davies sprinkled through the annals of Welsh International rugby history, that the feeling of playing for a family inside the 'family of Wales' has been so marked in the team's approach down the years.

Some confusion remains as to when the Welsh Rugby Union actually came into being. One school suggests a meeting at the Tenby Hotel in Swansea in 1880. Others subscribe to a similar gathering of clubs at the Castle Hotel in Neath on 12th March 1881. The game itself however had already firmly taken root in the preceding decade. The original 'big three'—of Cardiff, Newport and Swansea—all had substantial fixture lists in the 1870s then, as now, the other Welsh clubs which sprung up wherever there was space to kick and handle a ball in between the coal pitheads and belching iron-works, looked to them for guidance and inspiration. It was Cardiff who introduced the four threequarter lineup in 1885, a tactical development which helped to shift the emphasis of attack away from the old-style, repetitive forward rushes. It was a far-reaching change which was to influence the course of rugby history throughout the world.

Newport are unique in British rugby in that they are affiliated to both the English and Welsh Rugby Unions. This stems from the 400-hundred year old debate as to whether or not Monmouthshire, or Gwent as it is now, is part of England or Wales. With typical Welsh pragma-tism, Newport, as the main county town, opted for membership of both! Swansea were the pioneers of overseas club touring, going to France, Rumania and Italy long before the idea of spreading the gospel in this way had occurred to anyone else.

Like most other areas of the United Kingdom outside the catchment areas for the big public schools and universities in England, the rugby message was brought to Wales by returning students. The first Welsh XV that took the field against England at Blackheath on 19th February 1881 was soundly thrashed by the modern equivalent of 56-0. That side was made up almost exclusively of players with experience of rugby at either Oxford or Cambridge.

However, once the game seized the imagination of the working class, it spread like bushfire. There were several reasons for this. Despite its aristocratic beginnings in Wales, it rapidly became a truly classless game giving a miner's son as much public acclaim and social standing as that enjoyed by the offspring of an archdeacon or landowner. It was physically a very tough pastime and as such matched everyday living conditions. It gave the re-emerging Welsh nation a sporting chance, in every

Below: The electrifying speed of Gerald Davies made him unquestionably the world's finest wing in the 1970s. Davies possessed a bewildering side step off either foot which left countless opponents stranded. One of the great thinkers and (as befits a Cambridge graduate) an astute writer on the game he is, or was, one of Wales' greatest players.

sense of the phrase, of competing on level terms with the English. Not that that first International result gave much hope in the initial stages. Although Ireland were defeated in 1882, up until the turn of the century, Wales had only won 16 out of the 46 Internationals they had played. Then came the first of three 'golden eras'.

Between 1900 and 1912 Wales won the Triple Crown—defeating the other three home countries, England, Ireland and Scotland, six times. Indeed Wales went 22 home games before being defeated. The only side to win at Cardiff Arms Park in this period were the 1906 Springboks. The year before had seen the most celebrated International in Welsh rugby history, the defeat of New Zealand 3-0. This was the game of the disputed Deans 'try' which would have levelled the scores had the Scottish referee allowed it.

Those 12 years produced sporting legends like the two Bancrofts, Billy Trew and Percy Bush whose memory today is scarcely any dimmer than when they dwarfed the rugby world at the turn of the century. But fortune's wheel was to turn: between 1923 and 1926 only three out of 15 matches were won. Yet even in this period of gloom and despondency, the individual spark of genius failed to be extinguished: personalities included Wick Powell at scrum half, Wilf Wooller in the centre, Cliff Jones the first of what was to become a devastating line of aggressive, sidestepping fly halves. However, it was not until 1950, 39 years after their last success, that Wales again won the Triple Crown under one of the post-war years' most respected captains, John Gwilliam.

Since 1968 the Welsh team's record, barring a two-year hiccup between 1971 and 1973, has been a quite extraordinary one: Triple Crown winners six times; Grand Slam winners three times; 43 matches played, and only five lost. The blot on this outstanding record lies in the Welsh performance against overseas sides, both home and abroad. All five matches against New Zealand lost, the solitary match against South Africa in 1970 drawn, three wins and two losses against Australia. Like good wine, the Welsh don't seem to travel well!

The last two 'golden eras'—between 1968 and 1971 and from 1975 up to this present time—are not a result, as in earlier times, of haphazard luck allied to individual skill. In 1967 the Welsh Rugby Union took what was then considered by some other bodies to be a step towards professionalism by appointing a dynamic personality, Ray Williams, as Coaching Organizer. A former trialist—flanker Williams embarked on his task with crusading zeal, converting the doubters by the sheer force of his personal conviction of the corporate

Below: Who'd be a hooker? Bobby Windsor certainly would. One third part of the Pontypool front-row, which passed into Welsh and world folklore. He—together with his props, Graham Price and Charlie Faulkner—provided the team with a solid platform which brought Wales almost unbroken success throughout the seventies.

benefits of good coaching. Never one to stifle that most precious Welsh commodity, 'flair', Williams was unquestionably aided on his arrival by the winning performances on the field of the national team. Again Wales were in the forefront of UK rugby thinking by being the first to adopt a squad system of selection and training, a policy that gave them a head start on the other countries, who only followed suit over ten years later.

The strength of Welsh rugby lies in the fact that besides being good innovators, the players are exceptional imitators too. After watching their national side in action, either live amongst the 50,000 who squeeze into Cardiff Arms Park (now the National Stadium) or on television, the young men of Wales then turn out for the little village teams of Abercrave, Abercynon, Cwmgors, Cwmllynfell et al, fired by the desire to repeat the deeds of the Pontypool front row and such individual heroes as Terry Holmes, J. J. Williams and Steve Fenwick.

The real core of the game in Wales is found in these clubs, not just the 17 sides who are loosely termed senior or 'first class' The actual playing gap between the Cardiff, Swansea, Newport, Llanelli, Pontypridd and any one of a dozen or more of the better junior XVs is relatively small. Confirmation of this fact happens each year in the highly successful Welsh Rugby Union Challenge Cup. Begun in the 1971/2 season as a result of pressure and an element of frustration from the smaller clubs plus an increasing need to improve the financial straits of a Union committed to long-term development spending on the National Stadium, the Cup has become something of a Holy Grail for minnows. After the first couple of seasons when they were swamped by their more experienced and better organized bigger brothers, it is now rare indeed if no smaller club progresses as far as the quarter finals defeating at least one of the 'big fish' en route.

It is not stretching the comparison too far to say that the world reputation enjoyed by Welsh male voice choirs also helps to explain one of the reasons for Welsh success on the rugby field. Both reflect the national instinct for close harmony, the thrilling crescendo, the unity of attack and purpose and the ego-warming glory in doing something well in front of an audience.

Rugby players, even those involved with the smallest of village clubs, stand tall in the community. There is an unreserved admiration for the 'hard man' amongst the forwards. Their reputation precedes them wherever they play and the 'mano-y-mano' confrontation with the opposing Goliath is as interesting to the spectator as the match itself. I recall one such character. He played in the second row for Pontardulais, a hamlet some 15 miles from Swansea. A gentle, ever-smiling

Left: Mervyn Davies (in headband), tragically cut down by illness in 1976 when a virtual certainty to captain the 1977 Lions team to New Zealand. A tall rangy no. 8 his 6' 5" presence always ensured that Wales had at very worst parity at the end of lineouts. A superb defensive cover his work rate behind the Welsh threequarters was prodigious.

Above: Steve Fenwick has developed a reputation for coolness and place kicking infallibility at international level which has tended to obscure his other centre talents.

Fenwick is a superb linking passer of the ball and his defensive skills are so highly tuned that he invariably pops up to save Wales with a decisive tackle near their try line.

man of impressive physique, he sang a seraphic tenor at chapel on Sundays in the famous local choir. Twenty-four hours earlier he had been putting the fear of God into a nearby West Wales team with a display of controlled ferocity that would have earned him a jail sentence outside the confines of a rugby pitch. He was known simply as the 'Hatchet Man!'

Yet there are some flat notes spoiling the ensemble. Dirty play is on the increase, not only in Wales but throughout the rugby world. For all the pious efforts of the administrators and stronger referees to metaphorically stamp it out, the nature of the game itself tends to glorify the strong and exterminate the weak. The Welsh paradox is very much in evidence here. The average Celtic physique is perhaps the smallest of the four Home Countries and from a need to survive, let alone win, sprung Wales' most precious rugby talent, an endless conveyor belt of fast, elusive threequarters and half backs.

Welsh rugby is strong at the highest level because its grassroot rugby is subconsciously geared to pushing and encouraging promising youngsters upwards, first from the playgrounds of valley comprehensive schools,

through to youth and junior representative XVs, then second class clubs, on to the major ones, and finally the national side. Like the creation of a coral island, those individuals and clubs who prepare the way and provide the opportunity for advancement are used and left behind as the embryonic Gareth Davies or Terry Holmes makes his climb. Welsh rugby is a bit of a whirlpool. Players often gravitate swiftly from the slower backwaters of second class rugby to the fast-moving, heady centre at International level and return to the rim or even leap out of the pool almost as swiftly. 'One cap wonders' abound in the history of Welsh International football.

What makes Welsh rugby special and unusual, however, is that the 'star' never truly leaves the nest from which he emerged. So close-knit are rugby people in this corner of the UK that it is almost incestuous! An individual's successes are shared and enjoyed by all who have been in contact with him, even on the most superficial level. Because it is an amateur game, the big names of rugby are still a part of the daily pattern of life, although the degree of attention they receive often stops only just short of idolatry.

Keith Jarrett was not a 'one cap wonder', indeed he made nine appearances in all between 1967 and 1969 when he turned professional with Barrow, but his debut against England at Cardiff Arms Park on 15th April 1967, reflected precisely the dream of every rugby playing younster in The Principality. Wales defeated the 'old enemy' 34-21 with 19-year-old Jarrett, only four months

Left: Gareth Davies, the latest issue from the mythological Welsh side fly half 'factory'. Following Phil Bennett into the national team was a daunting prospect yet the Cardiff youngster slotted in smoothly from the word go. Like Bennett and before him Barry John, Davies is a superb line kicker and forms an effective link.

Above: The unerring boot of Barry John puts Wales on the attack again. The artistic flair of the handsome Welsh fly half reached its zenith during the British Lions tour of New Zealand in 1971. There his skills moved critics to crown him 'King' John. But he was more than just a marvellous allround kicker.

out of Monmouth School, scoring 19 of the points! Even more incredibly, it was his first complete game in the full back position. Young Jarrett had swiftly built a reputation as a strong centre threequarter for the Newport club, but his International selection was due almost solely to the fact that he was a goal kicker of extraordinary ability. He appeared nerveless in moments of stress and so the selectors took a gamble on playing him at full back to avoid disturbing the established midfield pair, Billy Raybould and Gerald Davies. How well their optimism was repaid! Besides converting all five Welsh tries and kicking two penalties, Jarrett became the first Welsh full back since Viv Jenkins way back in 1934 to score a try. And what a try it was—full of flair, power, youthful exuberance and determination. Wales were in the lead by a narrow margin (19-15) midway through the second half when Jarrett, standing some 12 metres inside his own half near the left hand touch line, gathered a kick by Colin McFadyean, the English centre. The standard full back riposte would have been a safe kick for touch as all his teammates were on the opposite side of the field, but Jarrett, to everyone's astonishment, gathered the ball on the run and without breaking stride, hared 60 metres down the touchline to cross unchallenged in the left hand corner, not far from the spot where Teddy Morgan had scored the historic winning try against the All Blacks in 1905. That was Jarrett—a meteor in the classic Welsh rugby tradition.

The Pontypool front row are part of Welsh folk-lore. They have even had a popular song written about them which, not surprisingly, reached a high place in the Welsh charts. The three men, Tony 'Charlie' Faulkner, Bobby Windsor and Graham Price are as inseparable off the field as they are on. They played their first International as a trio against France in 1975 and for the next four years, until a serious knee injury brought Faulkner's international career to what he would consider was a premature end at the age of 36, they appeared together in 19 Internationals. As a combined front row they have all the ingredients of invincibility. Faulkner, a black belt judo, is one of the most wily loose head technicians in the game. Rather spindly in the legs for a prop, Faulkner has massive shoulders which help him to give a rock steady platform for his hooker. Just how important is his contribution to the successful operation in this most crucial area of modern rugby was graphically illustrated when Faulkner flew out to New Zealand as a British Lion replacement during the tour of 1977. The undisguised joy of the other two members of the 'Pooler' front row

already with the team as original selections, showed in the improved results gained after his arrival.

Bobby Windsor is the second longest serving Welsh hooker of all time behind the legendary Bryn Meredith of Newport. 'The Duke', as he is affectionately known, has one of the sharpest senses of humour and quickest striking feet in the game. Another strong man in the purely physical sense, Windsor is also a gifted player in the loose and features in a supporting role in many Welsh tries.

The immensely powerful Graham Price at tight head prop completes this formidable trio. Without peer in his position, Price epitomizes the strong silent type. Those who have played opposite him for 80 minutes say it is an experience akin to being put through a mincing machine! Besides his sheer, colossal presence, Price is no slouch around the field either. He scored a spectacular running try against France in 1975 that would have made any self-respecting threequarter green with envy.

Inside the game the trio's standing is at pedestal level. Even the legendary Gareth Edwards, surely the world's most complete footballer, recalls his most satisfying moment in a 53-cap career, as follows. After

Below: To follow Gareth Edwards into the Welsh team meant almost certain unfavourable comparison. Yet somehow Terry Holmes who also stepped into Edwards' boots in the Cardiff team, not only survived but actually filled what had seemed a yawning gap in the Welsh side with his own brand of skill and determination.

one of his searing 50-metre touch kicks to relieve intense French pressure in 1978 at Cardiff, came a terse 'well done Gar' from Price as he trotted upfield to the lineout now deep in enemy territory.

Coached and motivated at club level by one of Welsh rugby's most engaging characters, Ray Prosser, the Pontypool front row may be on the point of breaking up, but their memory will live forever in Wales.

How long can Wales remain the leading United Kingdom rugby nation? My guess is for some time. Although some members of the present pack are getting on a bit, behind them are willing replacements, itching for a chance. People like hooker Alan Phillips of Cardiff, prop John Richardson, and Peter Morgan the exciting Llanelli threequarter, already being talked of in the West as another Phil Bennett, will not let their country down. That gives a clue to why Wales is what it is in a rugby sense. The result of a game really does matter to both players and spectators. It is this passionate approach that has helped produce and encourage so many magnificent Welsh rugby players, so often the backbone of touring teams playing all over the world.

It was the advent of the 1980s that gave these new aspiring internationals their first experience of the intense competitiveness of the Five Nations championship. Phillips and Richardson played with distinction and skill and were rewarded by being selected for the 1980 Lions tour to South Africa. The talented all-rounder Morgan was also chosen for this party as a utility back.

Below: Gareth Edwards' last try for Wales versus Scotland, National Stadium, Cardiff 1978. More words have been written and more pictures taken of this legendary Welsh scrum half than any other rugby player in the history of the game. Power, pace, committment, skill, they're all summed up in this splendid picture of the West Wales boy who became a household name the rugby world over.

Above: Phil Bennett for the early part of his career had to live in the shadow of Barry John but when he emerged he soon established a world-wide reputation of his own. Often accused of not using his marvellous jink and attacking potential to its full extent, the quiet and very popular Bennett, who also captained the Lions, set Welsh and international scoring records that remain unequalled to this day.

FRANCE
Always a romantic somewhere

Unlike the Anglo Saxon world, we in France do not argue about the origins of the game about which we share a common passion. We are content to deck with flowers the tombstone of William Webb Ellis in the ancient cemetery of Menton on the Côte d'Azur as our everlasting tribute to the man who is generally credited with having invented the game at Rugby School in Warwickshire, England. The man who took such a revolutionary step ended his life as an obscure clergyman who retired to spend his last days walking amongst the beautiful scenery of the South of France. Who could blame him? However, his death and

Below: A prematch scene in front of a clubhouse which was built in 1892 as the fashion of the players undoubtedly reminds you.

Right: Pierre Villepreux scored 133 points for France in 29 appearances between 1967–72. A tremendous kicker of the ball, some of his long range penalty successes have passed into the game's folklore. But he was more than just a good pair of feet. A fine reader of the game with brilliant positional sense and as one can see from the position of Mervyn Davies, the Welsh captain.

whereabouts of his burial remained a mystery until 20th January 1960. Since then, with the blessing of the whole of the rugby playing world, the French Rugby Federation have taken it upon themselves to keep his grave in good repair. Nothing can prevent we French from attaching a kind of romantic symbolism to this invisible bridge which irrevocably links France to the origins of the game itself. In a sense the French have always regarded themselves as rugby crusaders often producing a brand of play that brought gasps of wonder and astonishment from their opponents and spectators alike. A great passion for rugby football has grown steadily, particularly in the south where the streets of towns and villages empty completely as the population settle themselves in front of their television sets on International Saturdays.

The French Rugby Federation, however, show a fine disregard for history. Although their headquarters near the Opera in Paris release a steady flow of information about current players, referees and captains, it has precious little in its archives dealing with the origins and establishment of the game in France towards the end of the last century. Through the mists of time it is possible, however, to pinpoint the establishment of the Le Havre Athletic Club in 1872. It was the brainchild of a group of young Englishmen who had returned to live in France drawn perhaps by lingering historical memories of Henry V's triumphant capturing of the French kingdom back in the 15th century. In rugby terms the French have

Above: January 1909, a winter's day, in France and a moment of indecision in a line out during a game contested by two local clubs.

Below: The Bagneres full back Jean-Michel Arguirre in determined mood. His international career began against Australia in 1971. Renowned for his coolness and excellent positional play, his attacking flair often exploits the half opening in an opponent's defence. It may surprise some to learn that his French debut was made, not at full-back, but at scrum-half, as partner to fly-half Berot.

more than redressed their honour taken from them at Agincourt, Crecy and Poitiers.

The colours of the Le Havre club incidentally were appropriately the light and dark blues of Oxford and Cambridge Universities! The first specialist rugby club was again the product of English expatriates—'Taylors' in Paris which set up shop in 1877. With the establishment of the 'Union of French Societies of Athletic Sports', (USFSA), in November 1887, rugby really got itself organized in France with 14 teams being recognized, 13 based in Paris and the other a provincial side 'le Stade Bordelais'. 'USFSA' had been the brainchild of Baron Pierre de Coubertin, the man who was later to re-establish the Olympic Games. De Coubertin's burning idealism about the purity of the amateur sporting ideal led him to take an active part in putting rugby union on a sound footing. He refereed the first French Cup final between the Racing Club de France and Stade Français on 20th March 1892. The game took place at the Plaine de Bagatelle in the middle of the Bois de Boulogne. Naturally enough the Parisian clubs dominated in the formative years but the shift of rugby power to the south west of the country has been such that the last team from the capital city to win the Cup was the Racing Club back in 1959!

The good Baron would have been saddened by certain events concerning the development of the game in France, particularly the accusations of the paying of players made by the four British countries which led to France's temporary expulsion from the International playing field. In his chapter on the development of European rugby, Carwyn James has made an objective analysis about these unhappy times.

Since the centre of power gravitated away from Paris, the style and flavour of the game has changed too. Its importance in the other big cities of France has never been strong. It is primarily a game played and enjoyed in the medium sized towns and important villages where it has become a central part of the community's life. Citizens identify with the players who wear the colours of their town. It is very much a game of the people, unlike some parts of Britain where rugby is still recognized as the game of the privileged monied classes.

The same was certainly true of early French rugby but exactly why and when the game broadened its horizons and became virtually classless no-one knows for sure. For many years the boundary between association football and rugby football has been the Loire river. To the south are those who hold dearly to rugby as a way of life while in the north the game is swamped by soccer so that rugby as a sport is known mainly by whatever the French television service decide to screen. The

Below: Jean-Claude Skrela added a new dimension to French back row play during his international career which began against South Africa in 1971. A man who was always there at the breakdown, in style and effectiveness closely resembled that marvellous New Zealand flanker, Graham Mourie. He retired from the international scene in 1978.

Left: Jean Pierre Romeu was one of the most accomplished kicking fly halves the game has known. He landed 71 points in seven matches during France's 1975 tour to South Africa. Tall, long-legged, he deceptively appeared to be a lot slower than he really was. However, he played to his strength which was line kicking.

Above: The huge figure of Jean Pierre Bastiat usually dominated the tail of the lineout. Here he is in action against Wales jumping at no. 3! Surprisingly agile for a man of 6' 6", his commanding presence helped France to defeat Wales in Paris in 1978 directing his country to their first outright Championship since 1968.

FFR have come to live with the fact that there are ten association footballers to every one rugby player, although in the south west the proportion drops to five to one. But whereas top class French soccer has much of the removed elitism of the world's most popular game, rugby union in the Republic remains very much of the people, earthy! This is best illustrated by an allegedly true story which brought together in Béarn two teams from neighbouring valleys who were sworn enemies. The referee, alarmed by the free for all that quickly developed with neither side paying much attention to the whereabouts of the ball, decided to make an example of one of the players by sending him off. He thought again when the forward in question said, 'You can't send ME off, this field belongs to me!'

Like the soil, French rugby varies from region to region, town to town. There is the 'spare' style of Béziers who have played such a prominent part in the destiny of the championship, a resurgence of the Cathar spirit. Then there is the Bayonne region, with its steaming foundries, which give it a strong empathy with that other area which spawns great rugby players, the mining valleys of South Wales.

Owen Roe, the devoted disciple of the full blooded game as played in Wales, came to live at the confluence of the Adour and the Nive. He developed an affinity with the Aviron Bayonnais of the Forgues brothers. Aviron Bayonnais won a memorable victory over the

Parisians of the SCUF in the Cup Final of 1913 at Colombes. The final score 31-8 included seven tries to the victors, two against, a record that will not easily be equalled.

The lure and appeal of the club championship has always been paramount in France. Internationally in the time of Jean Prat, 1947 to 55, France moved towards her first Grand Slam—the beating of England, Ireland, Scotland and Wales in the same season. In 1953/4 at Colombes in front of 53,025 deliriously happy spectators, France won her first Five Nations Championship which they shared with England and Wales. Prat led by personal example, a typical native of Toyes—strong, cunning, indomitable, tenacious. Lucien Mias then led a French side which in 1959 could justifiably claim to be the strongest in the world, winning the Five Nations Championship as well as defeating Johan Claassen's Springboks. Mias was the son of a policeman. After training as a teacher he embarked upon a medical career at the age of 25 eventually setting up in practice in his adopted city of Mazamet. His place in French rugby history is assured as a man who welded together men of vastly different backgrounds and talents into a force that no country could ignore or take lightly.

The first Grand Slam eventually arrived in the 1967/68 season largely through the efforts of the Camberabero brothers, Guy at fly half and Lilian the scrum half. They were members of the La Voulte club on the right bank of the Rhône although they had originally come from Saint-Vincent-de-Tyrosse, a town on the main road between Bordeaux and Bayonne. It is not a place to catch the tourist's eye but this town has produced more International rugby players per head of its 5,000 population than any other in France. Not surprisingly the Camberabero brothers possessed an almost telepathic

Below: 'The Little General' scrum half Jacques Fouroux was a past master at all the tricks of the trade. His battle with Gareth Edwards of Wales at the National Stadium, Cardiff in 1976 was a classic. Here the Frenchman, aided by Rives, just beats Edwards for the ball in a game won by Wales 19-13.

Right: Robert Paparemborde the powerful and skilful S. Paloise prop forward still manages to get the ball away despite being tackled by the Irish scrum half John Moloney during the match in Paris in 1978 won by France, 10-9. In spite of his bulk, Paparemborde is a fine player in the loose.

Above left: The Boniface brothers Guy and Andre were both superb servants of French rugby in the 1950s and 1960s. This is Guy with a typically incisive run through the centre for his club St. Montois.

Below left: Jerome Gallion gets his line moving in the Paris match versus Wales, 1979. One of the fastest men off the mark in modern rugby, Gallion is an outstanding exponent of the running game.

Above: Walter Spangehero— one of the finest French forwards of all time was capped 42 times in both the 2nd row and back row. His international career began in 1964 against South Africa and ended in the 1973 season.

understanding of one another and the deadly accurate kicking of Guy turned many a match in France's favour.

The second Grand Slam, in 1976/77 coincidentally revolved around the efforts of another member of La Voulte and a scrum half at that; Jacques Fouroux or as he became affectionately known on both sides of the channel, 'The Little General'. Fouroux was not originally from the Rhône area. He is first and foremost a Gascon from Gers, showing all the petulance of the region. Fouroux was quick to recognize that modern International rugby is dominated by large mobile forwards who knit together with complete discipline. In partnership with a kicking outside half, Jean-Pierre Romeu, the diminutive Fouroux hustled and bustled around the base of the scrum with deadly effect, rather like a terrier yapping at the heels of a lion. The huge French pack gave him blanket protection so that the inadequacies of his somewhat short and slow service were rarely exposed. Tactically he was one of France's finest leaders and as a motivator of his men amongst the best too. Although the kind of rugby the French side produced under his leadership in the mid 1970s might not have been to every connoisseur's taste, he did help French rugby to rid itself of being erratic.

Jean-Pierre Rives the marauding flank forward learnt a lot working as he did in such close harness with Fouroux. A man who stepped rather reluctantly into the captaincy, he won his spurs in 1979 when leading the French side in New Zealand. Rives is an outstanding player, not just because of his rugby skills which are considerable, particularly in attack, but because his shock of blond hair make him an easy target for the eye. In company with Skrela and Bastiat, he made up perhaps the most effective back row in 20th century International rugby, each complementing the other like a balanced meal and accompanying wine. Rives plays the game with a romantic fervour, in some ways he's rather a throw back to the 1960s, but with the gradual acceptance of the coaching and squad training methods now established in France, Rives is also capable of blending his individual brilliance to the team's needs.

This is where the future of French rugby lies. Never to stifle the freedom of expression of the individual while accepting the need to methodically organize and plan. Not often in the past have we achieved the right blend and we may fail in the future. It is this quivering uncertainty that makes watching and supporting France one of the great sporting joys of life.

EUROPE
The rugby empire of France

Rugby was brought to Europe by the French: they were the original missionaries and they still dominate the scene in Europe. This was the inevitable result of action by the four Home Unions. In February 1931, concerned about the spread of professionalism, they reluctantly announced that fixtures with France, at all levels, would stop. This decision effectively blocked any British influence on the European game.

Relations were not resumed until two months before the war with Hitler's Germany, the decision being made at a meeting held in London on 7th July 1939. The irony of the situation was that the game in France had hardly changed; the better players still moved from the smaller to the bigger clubs for obvious reasons; and even in 1953 in Paris the Scots told the French Federation in no uncertain terms that if a former Rugby League player was not removed from their team they would return home immediately.

The main reason for 'the unsatisfactory condition of the game as managed and played in France' was the club championship, inaugurated in 1906 and therefore the oldest in the rugby world. It is so competitive that today playing in a championship winning club side ranks almost as high as receiving an International cap!

At this time the game was controlled by the Union des Societies Françaises de Sport Athletique. In 1920 it was replaced by the Federation Française de Rugby but not long after this takeover, 12 of the leading French clubs broke away to form the Union Française de Rugby Amateur. However, the hostile reaction of the British governing bodies acted as a great unifying force and they soon rejoined the Federation to preserve the rugby honour of a nation then ostracised by the British.

In 1939 the representatives of the United Kingdom Four Home Countries sent a letter specifying clearly the fundamental conditions which they expected of the French before they were readmitted to the fold:

'The real foundation of the game as played in our countries is the friendly match between clubs,' the

Right: Rugby in Italy was given a tremendous boost when the All Blacks played at Rovigo on their way home from their short tour of the United Kingdom, 1979. Although Italy lost 18-12, missionary visits like this are vital for the game's continuing development and expansion and to run New Zealand so close was quite an achievement.

letter went. 'It is not for the Four Unions to lay down whether or not league or club championships should be instituted or played for in other countries, but as a result of their lengthy experience and in the desire to be of assistance to the FFR they would tender the advice that the Federation would find that it would be more effective in the prevention of veiled professionalism and foul play if competitive rugby such as club championships were barred.'

The advice was not heeded. The club championship was never disbanded or even discouraged because the French clubs just wouldn't hear of it. However, a former great player and brilliant administrator M. René Crabos, in his capacity as President of the FFR, did a marvellous job in the 1950s by somehow preserving his country's club championship whilst maintaining France's overseas contacts despite the Anglo Saxon and Celtic disapproval from across the English Channel.

In recent times a similar situation has arisen in South Africa. With the breakdown in International relationships, the Currie Cup has assumed a far greater importance than ever before in the SA rugby calendar. In France, apart from the desire to spread the game throughout Europe, what really matters is the club championship. In Italy, too, most players prefer playing for their clubs in the championship to playing for their country.

What was good for the French was good for their neighbours in Europe. Twickenham has been the headquarters of the game the world over for English-speaking people, but for the Europeans Paris has been the fountainhead, certainly until recently. Yet there is a wind of change abroad as we approach the 1980s.

The only European nation capable of challenging the French at the moment is Rumania—conquerors of the best French national team twice in the last decade. Even Fouroux's 1978 team only scraped home by three penalties to two at Clermont-Ferrand: Fouroux's team

Below: Jacques Fouroux the French scrum half and captain getting his line going against Rumania in Bucharest 1976. This game, won by Rumania provided one of the biggest upsets in modern rugby. Afterwards the French admitted, 'we were over-confident and under motivated'. But the Rumanians continued to give them some close matches.

lacked the flair, the style and the panache typical of the French as we have known them and the inevitable stalemate resulted.

Rugby was introduced to Rumania at the beginning of the century by students returning from English and French universities. Based in Bucharest, the first Rugby club was known, for some contrary reason, as 'The Rumanian Tennis Club'. The club founded the first national championships in 1914 and, inevitably, won it for the first three seasons. But the game never really caught on until after World War II when other main industrial and university centres became interested. Places like Timisoara, Iasi, Cluj-Napoca—lovely names these—Petrosani, Brasov, Arad, Craiova and others. The Rumanians now claim that in the Black Sea port of Constanza and the industrial centre of Birlad, rugby has become even more popular than soccer.

A fascinating feature of their administration is that every town has its own knockout competition which gains the winners a place in the national championships. Since 1914, the main strength of Rumanian rugby has been in Bucharest and it has taken almost three score

years for an effective challenger to emerge. In 1972 the lecturers and students of the Timisoara University Club became the first provincials to win the championship of Rumania, while Constanza continued the momentum by winning three times in the last four years.

There are three Leagues in the Rumanian National Championships: the A League (16 teams), the B League (41 teams) and the Juniors (40 teams) and the number of registered players in Rumania now is more than 12,000. Leagues, leagues and more leagues at all levels. Mentally and physically the players are hardened by the competitive approach. As in the whole of Europe, friendly games, the essence of the amateur rugby spirit of enjoyment, are frowned upon and neglected by committees and spectators.

With a Ministry of Sport geared to the gathering of

Below: Not surprisingly France has played a leading part in the spread of the game throughout Europe. Here they are in action against the USSR who like most of the West European countries have tried to model their style of play on the French. Many of these developing countries saw the French as their passport to acceptance by the establishment.

gold in International competition, the Rumanians are single-minded in their pursuit of winning. Their formula, however, does not always produce a positive, winning policy but favours an approach towards not losing.

Playing for Swansea against Constructsia and Locomotiva (they are now known as RC Grivita Rosie, the Railway Factory Club) at the 23rd of August Stadium in Bucharest, 1954, I was amazed by the fitness, the command of the unit, the individual skills and the tactical awareness of both clubs. The outstanding Locomotiva player was their blond flanker, Viorel Morariu, who managed the Bucharest side in Britain in 1978 and the full national side in Wales the following season.

Whenever I stayed in Bucharest, I spent many hours discussing coaching techniques with the Rumanian coach, Ardhur Vogel, who had prepared a most scientific coaching manual entitled, *Rugbi—Tehnica, Tactica, Antrenament.* Vogel had gathered material from volumes published the world over. All Dr Danie Craven's published works, for instance, had been translated from Afrikaans into Rumanian!

Last season while coaching in Italy, I often came across Alex Penscui, a full back who played for Locomotiva and later for the national side on two occasions against Llanelli in Moscow in 1957. We discussed the Rumanian thorough physical preparation based on methods successfully adopted by the Russian Olympic athletes of the 1950s. He also admitted that the national squad often spends the occasional week or two limbering up by the shores of the Black Sea when an important match or tour is imminent. A high level of fitness is expected of each player.

There is no doubt that initially they learned the game from the French, but in recent years through more contact with the UK and the studying of films and television, they claim to have developed a style of their own. Gone, or more or less so, is the Latin flair and their approach now is more disciplined and certainly much duller.

When they paid their first visit to New Zealand in 1975, the year of their second victory over France, the Kiwis, themselves rarely bristling with excitement, accused the East Europeans of being too cautious! In eight matches they scored only 11 tries and later in their first two matches in Wales in 1979, against Ebbw Vale and Pontypridd they didn't score a single try.

I played for Llanelli in the Yonter (Peace and Friendship) Festival games in Moscow in 1957. It was a triangular competition, between Rumania, Czechoslovakia and ourselves. Jean Prat's French team were also there headed by René Crabos but they would not participate in the competition because we were only a club side. This did not prevent Monsieur Crabos from becoming a member of a 'jury' which sat in the middle of the stand. The captain of any team could stop the game and appeal to the jury if he disagreed with the decision of the referee.

We beat Czechoslovakia easily. They played a loose, basketball type of game. These days, although

only in the second division of FIRA, they are a much better team and well served by their coach, Eduard Krutzner. They play a more exciting game than Poland, a team managed by a gentleman called Scotland who speaks with a Scots accent so I'm told by Gwyn Evans who succeeded Roy Bish as the Italian national coach! The Poles are a tough lot, difficult to beat on their own ground, but have little as yet to offer to the world of rugby.

The Russians are different. We shall hear a great deal about them before very long. In 1957 there was

Below: The game has really taken root in Rumania. Their national team toured the United Kingdom in 1979 and gave the European Champions a real fright at Cardiff before losing 13-12. Here against France the drive and enthusiasm of the Rumanian pack puts Jean-Pierre Rives under pressure.

Right: Rumania v France, Bucharest 1976. This game was regarded by the French as a mere warm-up for the Five Nations International Championship. But they had a rude shock, losing 15-12 and then only narrowly defeating Australia in the first of two Tests.

little or no rugby played in Russia. Llanelli trained almost daily at the Metrostroi stadium in Moscow during a three-week stay and were watched by a group of interested observers who seemed to be taking copious notes of our sessions. 'Come back in twenty years,' they said, 'and we'll give you a good game.' Too true!

In the 1977/78 season the USSR Youth team gave a worthy performance in a tournament held in Parma, Italy; in the 1978/79 season the USSR gave a strong French team a run for their money. The following week they beat Italy who had already beaten the Pumas from Argentina, who had held a full England side to a draw at Twickenham! The Russians are strong, fit, athletic and they have learnt the basics well.

Rugby started seriously in Italy in Milan 50 years ago. Again the game is based on competition. There are a number of divisions and the *Scudetto*, the winning of the championship is what really matters. With 14 teams in the first division, 26 championship games to be played between October and May, it is a hard, long haul to win the Scudetto. Tough on the coaches since only one team

Above: Behind the Iron curtain, Rumania is the leading exponent of rugby football. The game has expanded rapidly since the war and regular matches against top class opposition, particularly France has speeded up the technical progress which now makes them a strong side.

Right: An attacking moment for the Italian fullback during their international match against New Zealand in 1979. The advancing All Blacks have been wrong footed by the number 15 giving him the option of running the ball away from danger or kicking for position—the Italians lost.

can top the League and 'nice guys who come second are not favoured in Italy.

Most of the best teams come from the north, the Veneto region. In the last few seasons the Scudetto has been won by Petrarca of Padova, by Benetton of Treviso and by Sanson of Rovigo. Most teams are sponsored. Sanson and Algida of Rome (coached for two seasons by Roy Bish) are ice-cream companies. They put a lot of money into sport and expect good results!

The Italians tend not to take their game as seriously as the Rumanians or the Russians. They enjoy playing far more than training and for this reason the committees like having coaches from abroad—people like Julien Saby of Grenoble, Roy Bish, Gwyn Evans, David Williams (Parma) and myself from Wales, Richard Greenwood the England flanker, James Stoffberg of South Africa. Pierre Villepreux one of the greatest ever French full backs became National Coach in 1978.

As in France and most other European countries, in Italy players are registered at the beginning of the season. They are given an identity card complete with photograph and before every match the referee inspects the cards and checks on the identity of each player. And if a member of the committee or the Coach wishes to sit on the bench, as soccer managers do, they too must produce an identity card.

Violence, a feature of French championship matches, is frowned upon elsewhere in Europe. At every game, a man is appointed to watch from the stand. If he sees the use of the punch or a boot which the referee hasn't spotted, a telegram may well arrive on the Thursday morning naming the culprit and a suspension will be given. Generally the standard of refereeing in Italy doesn't match the quality of coaching or playing.

Since the schools don't play in Italy, rugby is club-centred and tends to be a middle-class game. A club like Rovigo would have a mini-rugby section and then teams at all age groups up to Youth or Colt level. A group of about a dozen coaches on different afternoons of the week would coach about 250 youngsters. Gates vary. Small in Sicily, Reggio Callabria, and Rome but a few thousand would watch in Brescia, Parma or any of the clubs in Veneto. A play-off between Petrarca and Rovigo in 1976 attracted some 20,000 spectators.

The other feature of Italian rugby which is most important is that clubs at the moment are allowed two 'strangers' (stranieri). This has helped to raise the standard of play. Players of the quality of Andy Haden and Glyn Rich of New Zealand, Dirk Nande and Dreis Coetzer of South Africa and Robin Williams and David Cornwall of Wales amongst many others have contributed much to the well-being of the game.

It is, however, a great pity that the game is geared almost totally to the club championship. France lead and the others follow. France is still the power in the ruling body of Europe, FIRA, but I have a feeling, particularly now that France are members of the International Board, that the other countries in Europe would like to go it alone. Rumania would love to participate in the Five Nations Tourney but their chances just yet are minimal. After all, it took France three score years and ten to become members of the International Board.

France usually win the FIRA first division championship. In the 1978/79 season they gained 15 points, Rumania 13, Russia 11, Italy 9, Poland 7 and last Spain with 5. Mr. Morgan Thomas of Wales, the new Coaching Organizer of Spain, has much hard work ahead of him trying to organize the Federacion Espanola de Rugby. He can take heart however by looking at the rapid strides made by other European countries where the game has taken root. By the turn of the century, it may even begin to rival soccer!

SOUTH AFRICA
Out in the heat of the cold

Little did they realize what they were about those hardy, pioneering British and Boers. Little were they aware in those rugged few decades before the turn of the last century that the game they were just starting to play together was to become a great unifying factor in welding together into one nation peoples of vastly differing outlooks and beliefs. Little also did those self-same British and Boers perceive that generations later their offspring, both English and Afrikaans-speaking South Africans, would stand together bound firmly by the game of rugby in common defiance, rightly or wrongly, of world opinion, while at the same time pressing internally for acceptance of their right to play alongside black team-mates in tours to Britain and France. And this, more than 100 years later, is where South African rugby finds itself today; at a political crossroads.

Shown the way by new and seemingly more sympathetic national leaders, most white South Africans want nothing more in these enlightened times than the abolition of the dreaded apartheid laws that have bedevilled the country for the past 70 years. Politically enforced languishment in a sporting limbo has forced rugby in Southern Africa to turn inwards for survival. Sadly, the signs are far from healthy—either on the playing field and off—and so it is with ever-increasing desperation that Springbok rugby is turning to its traditional allies for a lifeline to the future.

The exact origins of the game of Rugby Football in South Africa are obscure, but it is generally held that the first games of note took place between regiments of the British Army doing service in the country at the time of the Zulu wars in the mid-1800s. What is certain is that the game was spread by Canon Ogilvie, who landed at Cape Town in 1858 from England to become headmaster of the Diocesan College there. However it was not until 1875 that the first rugby club as such, came into being. This was the Hamiltons, whose formation was followed the next year by the Villagers RFC and Gardens, three years later.

Right: The massive crowd looks on as Carel Fourie, with the ball tucked safely under his arm, leaves a Frenchman stranded on the ground and his fly half, Gerald Bosch, to his right, as he runs strongly, attacking the opposition during the first test the Springboks played against France in 1975.

.Other clubs soon sprung up, the most famous being that at Stellenbosch not far from Cape Town. Throughout the country, from the inland diamond fields of Kimberley and up the coast to Port Elizabeth and Durban, the game rapidly increased in popularity; provincial unions were formed to look after the interests of the clubs and to arrange competitions among themselves. Having first developed in and around Cape Town, Western Province became the first organized Union in 1883 and in 1889, the South African Rugby Board was constituted to oversee the development of the game on a national scale.

South Africa was then still a much divided country, with Natal and the Cape Colony peopled by predominantly British stock and the two republics of the Transvaal and Orange Free State belonging primarily to the Boers. Although the game naturally enjoyed greater popularity among the British, rugby matches were taking place in the Transvaal where a large number of British and foreign migrants had drifted in search of fortune on the gold reefs of Johannesburg and the Witwatersrand.

It was Cecil Rhodes who, in 1881, stood financial security for the first ever touring team from Britain to South Africa. This pioneering visit, under the captaincy of W. E. Maclagan, forged an alliance that was to outlast two Civil Wars, two World Wars and the demolition of the once-mighty British Empire.

At a luncheon on the day of the departure of the team on the *Dunottar Castle* on 20th June 1891, the founder and chairman of the Castle Line, Sir Donald Currie, handed MacLagan a handsome gold trophy to be awarded to the side that displayed the best performance against the touring team. And so the famous Currie Cup came into being, a trophy that today is the most sought-after prize in South African rugby.

Not unexpectedly, MacLagan's team swept all before them winning every match on tour scoring a mammoth 222 points to 1 in 19 games, including three Internationals. They came again in 1896, but in the intervening five years the stripling had learnt its lessons of the first tour all too well and not for another 55 years was a South African team destined to lose a Test series

With the war over and the process of uniting the Cape, Natal and the two republics of Transvaal and Orange Free State into one country well under way, Paul Roos in 1906 captained the first South African team, which came to be known as the Springboks, on a tour to Britain. With the formation of the Union of South Africa in 1910, now united under one flag, the mixture of Afrikaner and Englishman provided a firm foundation for the development of South African rugby at all levels of the game. And what a successful mixture it has proved to be—the tough, virile Boer farmers possess a near fanatical zeal, and when allied to the talents of fleet-footed, swift-thinking astute men from across the ocean the basics of the game are solidly forged with the emphasis placed on well-crafted forward play to secure a good ball for enterprising and swift-blooded backline runners.

This formula, simplistic though it well may be by modern rugby standards, proved more than adequate for Springbok teams to dominate the International scene for more than 60 years. 'Subdue and penetrate' were the key words by which all Springbok teams from the side captained by Roos in 1896 to the ill-fated, ill-chosen tour to New Zealand in 1956 were to stand and fall. The zenith of this golden era was undoubtedly the 1930s and more specifically, 1937. It was the Springbok team of 1937 that toured Australia and New Zealand under the captaincy of Philip Nel, a hardy farmer of Boer stock, that is generally regarded in the annals of South African rugby as the greatest of them all. Many of the most illustrious names in South African rugby came from that team and that era—Danie Craven, Boy and Fanie Louw, Benny Osler, Gerry Brand, Tony Harris, Louis Babrow, Ferdie Bergh, Dai Williams, Jan Lotz and Lucas Strachan were but some of them.

They were rugby immortals all, with Craven probably the most remarkable of them. He was destined after 16 Test matches in the Springbok green and gold including the captaincy at the age of 27 to become a selector, team manager, a member of the International Board and finally, in 1956, President of the South African Rugby Board, a position he holds to this day.

Famed for his dive pass and his half back link with Tony Harris in New Zealand in 1937, Craven is the grandson of a Yorkshire immigrant. He grew up in a Free State farming community and entered the rugged arena of International rugby against Wales at Swansea, emerging from that match with an indestructible reputation built on his sheer courage in the face of tough forward play. At the end of his Test career, Craven held a distinction probably unique in Test rugby by playing not only at scrum half but also at centre, fly half and at No. 8. He was and still is, a peerless rugby tactician.

After World War II and the sound drubbing of the 1949 All Blacks at home, Springbok rugby seemed headed for yet another golden era when the 1951/52 side under Basil Kenyon and Hennie Muller, with Danie Craven as manager, returned home from the British Isles having lost but one tour game to London Counties. In

the process they had notched up their biggest Test victory of all time—44-0 against Scotland at Murrayfield. More great Springbok names were emerging—Hennie Muller, the fastest and, by the reckoning of his critics, the most destructive No. 8 of all time, Chris Koch, Johan Claassen, Salty du Rand, Stephen Fry, Hannes Brewis, Tjol Lategan, and fliers of the likes of Paul Johnston and Tom van Vollenhoven.

Alas, it was not to be. Just four years after the

Below: The grand climax of the South African rugby season—the Currie Cup final. Here, the Springbok centre, Peter Whipp, playing for Western Province, in 1979, is perhaps trying to intimidate the opposition as he received the ball at full pace. Northern Transvaal were the opposing team that day and the game was played at Newlands in Cape Town.

Below right: Superb grace, balance and footwork as De Wet Ras, playing for Orange Free State, is poised to pass to his centre. The flanker is beaten, left trailing behind, and his opposing back comes rushing up from the right of the picture to challenge. The firm grounds in South Africa encourage beautiful, fast and flowing back play—at top speed.

triumphant 1951/52 tour of the British Isles, the Springbok bubble of invincibility burst on the rain-lashed, wind-swept fields of New Zealand in 1956 when a South African team surrendered its 60-year record. Since then Springbok rugby at International level has had its ups and downs, reaching an all-time low in the winter of 1972 when a mediocre England team that had just finished last in the Five Nations competition came and convincingly thrashed a South African Test team at Ellis Park 18-9.

Memories of the demo-plagued, unhappy tour of Britain in 1969/70 and the drubbing by England in 1972 were still fresh in mind when Willie John McBride's British Lions of 1974 defied the wishes of the British Government and landed on our shores. In between, the Springboks had convincingly hammered Brian Lochore's 1970 All Blacks, but you have to be a South African to appreciate fully the traumatic effects that shrouded an entire nation when the time came for the 1974 Lions to leave. The tears were copious when McBride's Lions returned home triumphantly unbeaten in 22 matches,

having routed the Springboks on their own turf three Tests to none with one drawn.

The day those magnificent Lions departed, South Africa was a nation in mourning for the lost art of rugby. Never before, since the first tour of 1891, had South African rugby experienced such humiliation. It was a humiliation born of complacency for had not the Springboks thrashed Lochore's 1970 All Blacks? Had not a mighty—or so we were led to believe—Springbok team undertaken another demo-ridden tour to Australia in 1971 to return home undefeated? England and 1972 at Ellis Park was just one of those things that can happen to any great rugby nation. Well, wasn't it? In the second Test played on the sun-parched highveld at Loftus Versfeld, Pretoria, McBride and his men had inflicted on the Springboks their biggest hammering ever in Test rugby. The score was 28-9! It was the darkest hour in South African Test rugby. From that day Springbok invincibility was reduced to nothing more than a fond memory. Some pride was salvaged when in 1976, Andy Leslie's All Blacks were beaten two Tests

Above: Robbi Blair, Springbok fly half, teeing up the ball for a goal kick against a World XV in 1977. The game celebrated the inauguration of the Loftus Versveld stadium. Blair is one of the current string of South African players with the ability to kick the ball enormous distances and with constant accuracy—a formidable player.

Right: Shortly to be starved of international competition South African Frik du Preez seized on the chance to play for the President's Invitation XV against England at Twickenham in a game staged as part of the Rugby Union's Centenary celebrations 1970/71. At du Preez's heels, former England centre John Spencer.

to one, although I, and many others, are still convinced South Africa was decidedly lucky to win that series, the last so far to be played by a Springbok team.

For South African rugby, the glory years are now over. Sad as it is for me to commit my feelings to paper, the Springboks at home or abroad, are no longer the major force they once were. The reasons for my conclusions are numerous. Without any doubt the greatest adversary faced by South African rugby over the past decade and more has not been the British Lions, the All Blacks or even the Tricolores, but rather the country's near-total isolation from the rest of the rugby-playing world. While rugby is still generally held to be the country's national sport—at least among the white sections of the population—and the fervour and the enthusiasm still run high in those centres where Currie Cup rivalries take place, the popularity of the game appears to be on the wane. The reasons are obvious. No longer are Springbok teams able to test their mettle against the Welsh, the Scottish, the English, the Irish, the All Blacks or the Wallabies in those countries.

From the time Springbok teams first faced demonstrators against South Africa's apartheid laws in Dublin and Christchurch during the tour in 1965 and again in Britain in 1969/70 and Australia in 1971, the vital international contact so necessary as a yardstick by which to measure a nation's prowess now barely exists. With traditional rugby rivals and allies falling by the wayside, it is inevitable that the standard of our rugby has become almost impossible to maintain or improve upon. McBride's 1974 Lions proved this in no uncertain fashion.

Further proof that interest in the game is waning at a rate that should be alarming the South African Rugby Board president Dr. Danie Craven can be gleaned from recent statistics which show no growth in playing numbers whatsoever. In 1970, when the last of the great Springbok tours overseas took place, there were 34,600 registered rugby players in South Africa. In 1978, the number had dwindled to 34,400—a net loss of 200, despite the increase in population.

Clearly the lack of overseas tours and the fast diminishing number of overseas International teams to South African shores is having its effect on the younger population who see no future in training long hours each week for recognition that now extends no further than provincial level. Inflation and other economic factors now hitting the pockets of all South Africa's young men, are playing their part, too. Already there is talk that South Africans should retaliate for its isolation by turning to professional rugby. And there are many rugby philosophers among us here who believe that pay-for-play is the only way the game will survive the 1980s.

As a result, much of the old joy has gone out of South African rugby. Always physical, the game is now far too robust. It has lost its flair and is almost totally reliant on kicking fly halves for winning points. Inevitably, this has led to the emergence of personalities such as Gerald Bosch, Robbie Blair, De Wet Ras and Northern Transvaal's Naas Botha, who today is referred to as

South Africa's Golden Boy of Rugby. Sadly, it is these robot-like, goal-kicking machines—they would be put to shame by the likes of Okey Geffin and the legendary Don Clarke—who are today the household names in South African rugby, much to the detriment of the game. With most teams now opting for the infamous ten-man tactical approach of forward domination and kicking fly halves in the belief that it is easier to score points this way rather than notching up tries with fleet-footed runners and sharper wits, it is small wonder that the game is fast losing its spectator appeal. Not even clubs of the stature of Cardiff, Newport, Llanelli and the North West Countires who toured here in 1979 drew the crowds they could have expected a decade or so ago.

The game has changed remarkably in other respects, too. Few of our sturdy farmers now take an active interest and today top club and provincial teams comprise mainly university students (Stellenbosch, Pretoria and Bloemfontein), national servicemen and policemen (Pretoria and Bloemfontein).

Another new facet in recent years in the all-devouring search for greater winning potential is the arrival on the scene of full-time professional coaches employed by the major provincial unions. Products of the same or similar coaching courses, these coaches all possess the same outlook on the game with the accent on forward play and, need I add, kicking fly halves. After all, does not the livelihood of these coaches depend on the results they produce? Gone, for all time it seems with

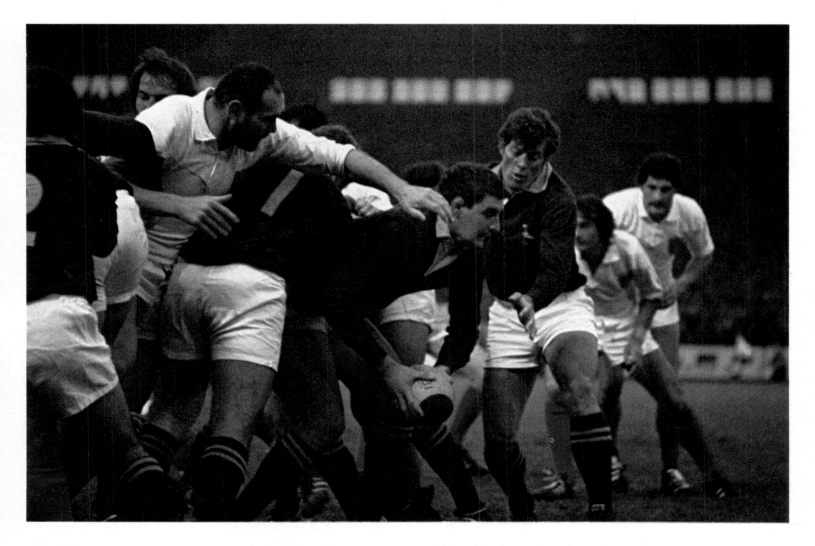

Left: Two giants of the past. Tommy Bedford with the ball, and looking on anxiously waiting for a pass, now South African ambassador to the United Kingdom, Dawie de Villiers. The two developed a superb partnership at the base of the scrum in the 60s, playing for the Springboks.

Above: Jan Ellis, to the left of the ball carrier, is another of the seemingly endless supply of quality back-row forwards produced by South Africa. The political situation restricted his appearances, but Ellis was never found lacking when involved in testing confrontations.

the death of the much-lamented Izak van Heerden, one of the greatest thinkers in modern rugby, is the complete 15-man approach to the game.

However much South African rugby has been drained of its former life and vitality by international isolation, one positive aspect has emerged. Through Peter Hain and his demonstrators the South African Government has been forced in the last decade to change its sports policies in drastic fashion but for the better. Though the enormous strides taken towards multiracial sport in South Africa over the past three to four years may not seem enough to the outside world, the fact is that black, white and coloured are today playing happily together in most sporting codes. Should this integration continue at the same pace as rugby grew in leaps and bounds when first introduced to the country last century, the game here could well experience a new and much-needed lease of life in the years ahead. If all the three separate controlling bodies of white, black and coloured rugby could be brought together ultimately under one controlling wing, enormous benefits would accrue to all rugby players in this country. Perhaps then we would be accepted back into the international arena which we are so sorely missing.

Any attempt to single out two contemporary South African players deserving of the description of greats is a forbidding exercise in view of what has taken place over the past decade. Since the retirement of Frik du Preez, only two forwards come to mind. They are the current Springbok captain and No. 8, Morne du Plessis and flanker Thys Lourens. For both their playing ability and qualities of leadership these two can hold their own among the great Springbok No. 8s and flankers of all time. South Africa today knows no more popular player than the courageous Lourens, who made his first of only three appearances for South Africa in 1968. Now, at 36, he still commands the course of Northern Transvaal in its bid for its tenth Currie Cup in 13 years.

In closing, special mention should be made of the role played in contemporary South African rugby by Gerald Bosch whose appearance and goal-kicking feats in the No. 10 jersey for Transvaal and South Africa paved the way for the round-the-corner goal kicker. Few other players in South African rugby history have dominated the outcome of a game more than this prodigious points-grabber whose kicking shattered all South African rugby-scoring records and led to the birth of the kicking game as we know it—to our cost—today.

NEW ZEALAND
Tough, ambitious and dominant

Only once or twice in its 110 years of existence has rugby in New Zealand been troubled by controversy and diminished by critical debate. Marching into its twelfth decade, the game, as a recent Governor-General of the country remarked, has been turned from THE national pastime into A national one. During great tours such as that so brilliantly led by Graham Mourie through the British Isles in 1978, the old patriotic fervour is aroused. Then more than 70 percent of the country's total population of 3,100,000 watched direct telecasts of the great matches during the unholy hours of two to five on Sunday mornings. At other times, fervour wanes. The moral issue of sporting associations with South Africa, especially in rugby, is stirred by anti-apartheid activists. Administrators wring their hands and utter soothing platitudes about the incidence of violence in play and coincidentally a proportion of young parents determine that their sons will not play a game which puts teeth, limbs and sometimes heads at risk. Recently iconoclasm, the sport of knocking cherished institutions, including personalities, has been indulged to a degree unthinkable

Above: A rare illustration of the first Maoris touring team to travel to the British Isles in 1888–1889 season. They beat Ireland 13-4, but lost the matches against Wales and England.

Right: The most famous sporting war dance in the world: The Haka. Strangely the All Blacks rarely perform this Maori chant before a home Test match, but overseas, the tradition can send shivers of expectancy and apprehension through the minds of spectator and opponent alike.

breast, set off for New South Wales and an itinerary of eight matches. All were won and the New Zealanders' score of 167 points to 17 testified to the quality of the side.

The year 1888 was climactic. In April and early May and again in September and early October, a British team—originally captained by R. L. Seddon of Broughton Rangers, who was tragically drowned while sculling on the Hunter River in New South Wales and replaced by A. E. Stoddart of Blackheath—played 19 matches in eight centres for a record of 13 won, four drawn and two lost. New Zealanders had understood that they were not permitted to pass the ball—it has often since been alleged that they have never learned to do so!—but at the sight of the British moving it around, they reacted with joy. After this tour, a private promoter named Tom Eyton organized a 26-strong team, all New Zealand born, 22 Maoris and four whites captained by a Maori, James Warbrick, for the most arduous tour in rugby history. Including nine matches in New Zealand, two en route in Melbourne, 74 in the British Isles, 14 on a return visit to Australia and eight in a farewell trip around New Zealand, no fewer than 107 matches were

played. A scrum half named Paddy Keogh became the first national rugby hero.

In 1892, the New Zealand Rugby Union was formed. At the first annual meeting, it was resolved that the national playing uniform should be a black jersey with silver fernleaf, white knickerbockers and black stockings and it was in this colouring that the first official New Zealand team, the side of 1893, was sent to Australia. In 1905 came the great event which established rugby conclusively as the sport of New Zealanders and which established the All Blacks as world figures and leaders. A team captained by David Gallaher lost only to Wales in a programme of 33 matches in the British Isles and France. The overall score was 868 points against 47. Billy Wallace, who played pretty well anywhere in the backline, scored 230 points, only nine of them, be it noted—and he was a specialist place kicker—from penalty goals, while an inside centre, Jimmy Hunter, reputedly no sprinter, corkscrewed his way to 42 tries. Altogether, the team scored 100 goals, 115 tries, two drop goals, one goal from a mark and only four—count them—penalty goals. All New Zealand was enthralled. They were no longer curious country

---

Below: One of the all time great scrum halves Sid Going in action during the Maoris v British Lions at Auckland, January 1977. With his tactical kicking and rapier like bursts around the base of the scrum, Going was probably the most influential player on the New Zealand pattern of play in the 1970s. The style changed with his departure.

Right: The classical tackle by Mark Taylor on Noves of France. For the first 20 post war years All Black strength had been centred around huge mobile forwards complemented by kicking scrum halves. But players like Taylor, Bruce Robertson, Grant Batty, Bob Burgess and Stuart Wilson have emerged behind the scrum to shift the balance of power.

cousins from the colonies. They were kings of the game!

The Second All Blacks, as they came to be called, who toured to the British Isles and France in 1924 were unbeaten in their 30 matches, in which they scored 721 points to 112: 77 goals, 98 tries, three drop goals and only ten penalty goals. They were christened 'The Invincibles'. Although their tour record was smudged when one of their forwards, Cyril Brownlie, was ordered from the field for kicking a man in the International against England, they were very deeply cherished. Their full back, a 19-year-old Maori named George Nepia, was immortalized when he played in every one of the 30 matches. He remains the nonpareil among full backs.

It is saddening that those great golden days have been succeeded by occasions of violent combat in International competition and the continuous controversy over the South African relationship. During the 1960s, largely because of the influence of a supremely talented captain in Wilson Whineray, New Zealand topped the world, beating the Lions, Springboks, Australian Wallabies and, not least, Barbarians. This was the era of Colin Meeds, the unforgettable 'Pinetree', of Wake Nathan, 'The Black Panther', and Don 'Camel'

Clarke, who in 31 Internationals scored 207 points, almost half of them from penalty goals. The pack was dynamic, the backs were efficient, success was constant. But the 1970s brought defeats both at home and abroad by Lions, Springboks, Wallabies and, not least, French teams. In this fractious decade, New Zealand suffered more than at any other time in its history.

Many wounds were self-inflicted. Parochialism eventually turned too many provincial matches and, for that matter, club and school fixtures, into internecine warfare. An All Black scrum half, Chris Laidlaw, who later captained Oxford to the defeat of the 1970/71 Springboks in the first match of their tour of the British Isles, wrote a book, *Mud In Your Eye*, which witheringly damned many aspects of New Zealand rugby, both players and administrators. The book sold 25,000 copies, an amazing number for so small a community, proof of the indignation seething among the concerned section of the rugby public.

The conflict between the game's ruling council and those outside the pale became, as it still is, a matter of most serious concern. New Zealand rugby seems unable to escape the miseries of wretched controversy. Pelion

piled upon Ossa. It was gratifying that the Council's well-acclaimed decision to refuse tours of South Africa unless Maoris and/or other non-white players were eligible for selection yielded the presence of no fewer than five Maoris, including the great scrum half Sid Going and the superb threequarter Bryan Williams, who is part Samoan, in the All Black side which toured there in 1970. Yet when the Council, supported, to be fair, by most in New Zealand rugby, sent Andy Leslie's team there in 1976, the consequent walkout by 29 Black African nations from the Montreal Olympics provoked bitter criticism. It was symptomatic of the troublous times that two tours to the British Isles were tarnished by censure and sensation, the first occasion being the banishment of the prop forward Keith Murdoch from the tour of 1972/73 and the second the ruthless raking of the great Welsh back J. P. R. Williams while he was captaining Bridgend against Mourie's team in 1978. Welsh—New Zealand relations, always tetchy since an All Black centre Bob Deans was refused the try which would have drawn the fateful final International of the 1905 team's tour, plummetted to their lowest-ever level after the Williams' incident and raised the possibility that the New Zealand Union might veto the invitation for an All Black team to celebrate the centenary of the Welsh Rugby Union in 1980/81 with a tour.

Happily, the great grip of rugby on New Zealanders and the profound love of the game which has been the consistent and dominating factor since Charles Monro's time have been strengthened by the efforts of two specially fine players. Graham Mourie, largely because of television, made an international impact when with his leadership the All Blacks of 1978 brought off for the first time the winning of the Grand Slam by defeating Ireland, Wales, England and Scotland. For all that, he looked a sight too slim by modern standards to rank as a great flanker. Mourie overcame the apparent disadvantage by inexhaustibly chasing every man and ball. Because of his immense work rate, he brought off remarkable feats. He was extraordinary in his knowledge of law and at times expertly debated points with international referees. Yet he never complained about questionable decisions and when speaking publicly conveyed the true and simple sincerity of a modest man. Above all, he commanded by example. Ireland going into injury time were pressing hard at 6-6. Mourie wound up his men. With brilliance, Donaldson ran the short end of a lineout from scrum half and the hooker Dalton scored. Again, Wales were leading 9-0 and later 12-4 and had more than 40,000 singing to them on

Below: Rugby union is the one sport where New Zealanders feel a sense of superiority over neighbouring Australia. Here in a line out during the first Test at Wellington, Frank Oliver beats Garrick Fay to the jump and palms the ball back to his scrum-half. The match, closely contested, was won by New Zealand 13-12.

Right: Graham Mourie, the All Black captain, taking a rare breather during the international v France 1979 won by France 24-19 on Bastille Day. A quiet man both on and off the field Mourie's influence has been a telling factor in their overall success. A man who leads by personal example with an uncanny knack of being on hand when needed.

the Arms Park: they could not possibly lose. Yet again did Mourie lift himself into a higher gear, taking his men with him. While the circumstances of New Zealand's win by 13 to 12 provoked seething debate, none could deny the force of Mourie's example. All of Murrayfield was gripped when Scotland seemed certain to be going for a draw at 12-12 in the last International, but once again the Mourie magic worked. At the death rattle the All Blacks steamed to a try and victory by 18 points to 9. It was not to be doubted that Mourie fairly established himself with Gallaher, C. G. Porter of the Invincibles and Whineray among New Zealand's greatest captains.

After Stuart Wilson had toured to the Argentine in 1976 with a second-string All Black team, it was remarked that New Zealand had a great threequarter in the making. With his pallid complexion and shock of fair, gingery hair, Wilson was a distinctive figure, the more so because his white legs, an unusual feature in a country where so many spend so much time out of doors, could move very rapidly indeed. Wilson was also unusual among New Zealand players, if not all Inter-

national players of these modern times when victory is so important, in having natural humour—he was a merry fellow who seldom moped mum. At the Arms Park, playing Cardiff in 1978, he startled all in the great new stand by scoring a superb try of which the features were juggling with the ball held in both hands in front of him and subtle movement into and away from the likely tackler who waited for him but a whiff from the corner-flag. Again, at Swansea, facing West Wales one match later, Wilson stood out with two tries, the second one as dextrous as his Cardiff coup. Because they were beaten, and well beaten, by Munster a couple of games later, the All Blacks sadly shut up shop on wide-ranging attacking runs and Wilson perforce had to play itty-bitty parts far beneath his capacity and potential. But at the Arms Park again, in the key match against Wales in which the Welsh controlled at least 70 percent of the play, Wilson was once more an arresting figure, partly because of his swift following for a try of a kick-ahead by Osborne from midfield but even more because of his part in the first move of the game. Wales, kicking off, intended a two-man test from the first lineout deep inside the All Black quarter and calculated an early penalty with a garryowen, or even better, a try which would shatter the New Zealand morale. It was a good plan. It might have done the trick. But Wilson, making the catch within his quarter, confounded all plans by a searing run through midfield. The ball went into touch at about halfway, or in Welsh territory; and, said Bobby Windsor, 'that fixed us'. Wilson, the deerfoot, had shown yet again that in the best New Zealand rugby footballers are displayed many of the finest, most memorable qualities of the game.

AUSTRALIA
Pulling away strongly

The origins of organized rugby in Australia parallel those in the UK. There are mentions of a kind of 'football' being played early in the days of the colony, which was founded in 1788, but rugby as we know it was introduced by visiting units of the Royal Navy who had regular games against the resident British military garrison. Australia's oldest existing rugby-playing institution is the Sydney University Football Club, established in 1864. The original club as such was the famous 'Wallaroos' set up in response to a newspaper advertisement inserted by a Mr Montague Arnold in 1869. Such was the strength of the Wallaroos in those early days that they normally played with 15 men a side when 20 was the accepted number. The Southern Rugby Union, predecessor of the NSW Rugby Union, was established in 1874, just three years after the Rugby Football Union, whose rules it adopted.

A variation to the rules of rugby football was to develop in the adjacent colony of Victoria. Originally known as Victorian Rules, and later as Australian Rules Football, it was to have a huge longterm significance on the playing of the various football codes in Australia. It started in the Victorian goldfields in the 1840s, where a Mr Thomas Wills, who was born in NSW but educated at Rugby School, became disturbed at the lack of fitness of Victorian cricketers. He felt that a football-type activity not quite so strenuous as rugby, was desirable during the winters to keep the State's cricketers in shape. The new rules were introduced in a game billed as the 'Great Football Match', held at the Melbourne Cricket Ground in 1858 and grew to dominate the football scene in all Australian States except NSW and Queensland. In the process, it alienated approximately 65 percent of the Australian population from rugby! It now enjoys massive publicity and draws huge crowds who display an almost religious club fervour. It is interesting to note some similarities between current Australian Rules football and the kind of rugby played in England during the early years. For example, a player taking a

Right: Australian rugby came of age in 1978 when they defeated Wales 2-0 in the Test series in Australia. There had been isolated victories over other international sides in the past but it was the manner in which the Australian XV destroyed the European champions. Here flanker Greg Cornelsen breaks through with the Welsh defence in disarray.